365 REASONS YOU'RE THE PERFECT DAD

First published in Great Britain in 2005 by
Spruce, an imprint of Octopus Publishing
Group Ltd
Carmelite House
50 Victoria Embankment
London EC4Y 0DZ
www.octopusbooks.co.uk

An Hachette UK Company
www.hachette.co.uk

The authorized representative in the EEA
is Hachette Ireland, 8 Castlecourt Centre,
Dublin 15, D15 XTP3, Ireland
(email: info@hbgi.ie)

This edition was published in 2026

This material was previously published as
1000 Reasons You're the Perfect Dad

Design copyright © Octopus
Publishing Group 2005, 2026
Text copyright © Rebecca Hall 2005, 2026

Distributed in the US by
Hachette Book Group
1290 Avenue of the Americas,
4th and 5th Floors
New York, NY 10104

Distributed in Canada by
Canadian Manda Group
664 Annette St., Toronto,
Ontario, Canada M6S 2C8

All rights reserved. No part of this work
may be reproduced or utilized in any form
or by any means, electronic or mechanical,
including photocopying, recording or
by any information storage and retrieval
system, without the prior written
permission of the publisher.

Rebecca Hall asserts the moral right to be
identified as the author of this work.

ISBN: 978-1-84181-654-8
eISBN: 978-1-84181-662-3

A CIP catalogue record for this book is
available from the British Library.

Printed and bound in China.

10 9 8 7 6 5 4 3 2 1

Publisher: Lucy Pessell
Designers: Isobel Platt &
Kathrine Anderson
Senior Editor: Tim Leng
Assistant Editor: Samina Rahman
Production Controller: Allison Gonsalves

365 REASONS YOU'RE THE PERFECT DAD

hamlyn

In the twenty-first century, the role of fathers is less clearly defined than it used to be, say, fifty years ago.

Back then, the stereotype was that men went out to work to provide for their families, left the nurturing of children to their wives, and got together with 'the guys' every now and then to watch or play sports. Now there are no fixed rules. Men can be full-time single fathers or every-second-weekend fathers; they can be the parent who stays at home with young children or the extraordinary step-dad; and they are often the chief confidant, cook, and comforter in the household.

Of course, there have been men in every generation who realized the life-enhancing, eye-opening, benefits of having a close relationship with their offspring, but these days, as the media increasingly portrays this kind of dad, more and more men are discovering fatherhood's joys.

As well as loving them unconditionally, the perfect father befriends his children, shares their interests, and frequently gets down on the floor to play with them. A good father gives his children the ability to approach the world with confidence, expecting to be liked by everyone they meet.

Fathers across the planet and throughout the centuries have certain things in common, despite their cultural and religious differences. We all share the biological instinct to protect and the human desire to make our children happy. The very best fathers go further than this, aiming to inspire their kids to be the most fulfilled, exceptional people they can possibly be.

This collection aims to let perfect fathers everywhere know that their achievements have not gone unrecognized.

Why not tell your dad all the reasons why he's perfect today? You can go back to taking him for granted again straight afterward!

You've understood from the start that a child is not a possession, but a gift.

YOU'VE GOT A HUGE PERSONALITY, AND A GREAT BIG HEART TO MATCH IT.

Since I grew up and started seeing you as a person in your own right as well as my dad, my love for you has become much deeper.

> I know that there's nothing I could do that would make you stop loving me.

I'M SO GLAD YOU WERE THERE WHEN I TOOK MY FIRST STEPS IN LIFE.

I always feel my spirits lift when I know I'm coming home.

You never believed that affection was unmanly.

You always clapped the loudest at my school plays and cheered the loudest at my sports games.

YOU TAUGHT ME TO DEMAND HIGH STANDARDS FROM PEOPLE WHO SAY THEY LOVE ME.

The pride on your face when I brought home my report card, no matter what it contained, made me proud of myself and determined to do my best.

You relished every moment of my childhood.

THE MILESTONES OF MY CHILDHOOD SEEM TO BE IMPRINTED ON YOUR MEMORY.

YOU ALWAYS LIKE TO TELL OTHERS ABOUT MY ACHIEVEMENTS.

You worked so hard to give us the best things in life, and tried so hard never to let us see how tired you were.

YOU ALWAYS MADE ME FEEL THAT YOU WERE SO THANKFUL TO HAVE ME.

You still love me, even when I'm being awful.

You helped me see the strength and comfort that could come from a loving family.

I like to look at your capable hands and remember all the things they do for me.

YOU DROP EVERYTHING THE MINUTE YOU KNOW THAT I NEED YOU.

I always felt that you'd move heaven and earth to protect your family.

You're a jack-of-all-trades and master of quite a few.

> I feel so lucky to have you on my side, rooting for me.

I STILL REMEMBER THE FEELING OF MY SMALL HAND IN YOURS, AND HOW IMPORTANT IT MADE ME FEEL.

YOU ALWAYS MADE ME FEEL LIKE A PRECIOUS GIFT THAT YOU WERE LUCKY TO HAVE.

You took real pleasure in even the smallest of my achievements.

Everything you gave to me is part of me forever.

I treasure all my photographs that show the two of us together.

He caught the first accents that fell from thy tongue, And joined in thy innocent glee.

MARGARET ANN COURTNEY

I'M SO GRATEFUL THAT I GOT THE BEST FATHER ANYONE COULD HAVE.

YOU COULD ALWAYS MAKE ME LAUGH THROUGH MY TEARS.

I HOPE I CAN PASS ON TO MY KIDS EVEN A FRACTION OF WHAT YOU'VE GIVEN TO ME.

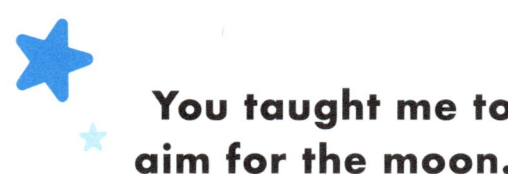

You taught me to aim for the moon.

I find myself becoming more like you as the years go by.

You always had enough time and energy for all the family, so that no one felt anything other than loved by you.

One of my greatest debts will always be to you, because you never made me feel as though I owed you anything.

All the feeling which my father could not put into words was in his hand – any dog, child, or horse would recognize the kindness of it.

FREYA STARK

You taught me the meaning of the words 'unconditional love.'

You made me realize that being a parent is about love and understanding, not control or expecting the impossible.

LOVE TO YOU HAS ALWAYS MEANT TIME SPENT WITH THE PEOPLE YOU CARE ABOUT.

Your main source of inspiration and motivation was always your family.

You never cared if we were the best, only that we were the best we could be.

You never minded getting your good clothes dirty when a grubby kiss was offered.

I have so many unforgettable memories of our crazy, funny times together.

> **If anyone failed to see my potential, you didn't hesitate to point it out.**

You showed me continual affection, even when I pretended to resist.

Some of the things I value most about you are your little, nameless acts of kindness.

It doesn't matter who my father was; it matters who I remember he was.

ANNE SEXTON

I HAVE A PHOTO OF YOU HOLDING ME AS A BABY THAT DEMONSTRATES HOW MUCH I MEANT TO YOU RIGHT FROM THE START.

I'LL NEVER BE TOO OLD FOR ONE OF YOUR BEAR HUGS.

> No one else cares about me the way you do.

ALL YOU WANT

IS FOR ME

TO BE HAPPY.

To her the name of father was another name for love.

FANNY FERN

You never missed an opportunity to say you were proud of me.

Although I dismissed so many of them at the time, your words often come back to comfort me.

YOUR PRAISE MEANS MORE TO ME THAN ANYONE ELSE'S.

YOU TOOK PLEASURE IN MY FIRST LOVE, AND THEN MY NEXT, NEVER BELIEVING THAT YOUR SPECIAL PLACE IN MY HEART HAD BEEN USURPED.

You always helped me see magic in the little things.

You know me back to front and inside out.

YOU MADE ME FEEL SAFE BEING THE PERSON I AM WHEN I AM WITH THE PEOPLE I LOVE.

You were never afraid to let me see how deeply you felt.

YOU TAUGHT ME THAT WE'RE ALL JUST PASSING THROUGH, AND TO VALUE EVERY SECOND WE GET.

There are some special things you've said to me that I'll treasure in my heart forever.

There's a certain way you look at me – half smile, half serious – that's just brimming with love.

I like it that you choose to be with me whenever you have some time to spare.

YOUR CONSTANT LITTLE DISPLAYS OF AFFECTION HAVE ALWAYS LED ME TO BELIEVE THAT I AM LOVABLE.

It is not flesh and blood, but heart which makes us fathers and sons.
FRIEDRICH SCHILLER

You actually worried that you weren't a good enough dad, when you were head and shoulders above anyone else I knew.

THE FACT THAT YOU MISSED ME SO MUCH WHEN YOU WERE AWAY MADE ME FEEL INCREDIBLY LOVED.

You're my touchstone for all that is wise and good and true in the world.

YOU HAVE AN UNCANNY KNACK OF MAKING EVERYONE AROUND YOU FEEL AS THOUGH THEY ARE THE FAVOURITE.

You never just assumed I would love you, but worked to make sure I did.

You believed in a better world, and fought to make it a place in which you would want your child to live.

FATHERHOOD BRINGS OUT THE BEST IN YOU.

You can remember every detail and all the emotion of the first time you held me in your arms.

YOUR LOVE FOR ME WAS NEVER SECRET – YOU ARE PROUD TO DEMONSTRATE IT TO THE WORLD.

You told me that having a child changed the whole universe for you, and that nothing was ever the same again.

YOU MAY NOT HAVE BEEN FAMOUS OR SET WORLD RECORDS, BUT TO ME YOU ARE A HERO.

When I first realized that you were a man, not a god, and that you had weaknesses too, I loved you even more.

My father would pick me up and hold me high in the air. He dominated my life as long as he lived, and was the love of my life for many years after he died.

ELEANOR ROOSEVELT

**You admired me with your heart
and loved me with your mind.**

> **YOU TAUGHT ME THAT
> TRUE WEALTH IS BEING
> SURROUNDED BY
> PEOPLE YOU LOVE.**

You gave me wings to soar into
my own space and life, but
I always knew where home was.

It's only when you grow up, and step back from him…that you can measure his greatness and fully appreciate it.

MARGARET TRUMAN

I love you right down to the very last detail – the set of your eyebrows, the look of concentration on your face, the shape of your ears, and the scent of you.

When a child, my dreams rode on your wishes, I was your son, high on your horse.

STEPHEN SPENDER

SECRETLY, YOU BELIEVE THAT I'M BETTER THAN EVERYONE ELSE IN THE WORLD — AND I THINK THE SAME ABOUT YOU.

You let me go my own way even when it wasn't what you wanted for me.

I love the way you treasure those awful photos from my childhood that show me with goofy haircuts and dreadful clothes.

When I was a boy of fourteen, my father was so ignorant I could hardly stand to have the old man around. But when I got to be twenty-one, I was astonished at how much he had learned in seven years.

MARK TWAIN

YOU UNDERSTAND THAT I HAVE MY OWN THOUGHTS AND OPINIONS, AND YOU NEVER TRY TO SECOND-GUESS THEM.

YOU DIDN'T EXPECT ME TO BE LIKE YOU, BUT I THINK YOU ARE PLEASED THAT, IN MANY WAYS, I AM.

My father was a statesman; I'm a political woman. My father was a saint. I'm not.

INDIRA GANDHI

YOU DIDN'T MAKE ME FEEL THAT THERE WAS AN IMAGE OF PERFECTION I HAD TO LIVE UP TO.

I sometimes see a wistful expression on your face and realize that you fear losing me.

For thousands of years, father and son have stretched wistful hands across the canyon of time, each eager to help the other to his side.

ALAN VALENTINE

You never treated my achievements as your own, but made it clear that they were mine, and due to my efforts alone.

It is a wise father that knows his own child.

WILLIAM SHAKESPEARE

I ASK YOUR ADVICE FIRST, BEFORE I TURN TO ANYONE ELSE.

You understood when I didn't want to talk, and you let your silence comfort me.

You're one of the wisest people I know – even though sometimes, you hide it well.

WHEN I SEEK YOUR APPROVAL, IT'S BECAUSE I VALUE YOUR OPINION.

You taught me how to laugh at myself

YOU ALWAYS PRETENDED THAT THE GIFTS I GAVE YOU WERE MORE TREASURED THAN ANYTHING ELSE.

It is admirable for a man to take his son fishing, but there is a special place in heaven for the father who takes his daughter shopping.

JOHN SINOR

> You've always accepted me as I am, but you've also always known my potential.

YOU ALWAYS KNEW WHAT I NEEDED WHEN I DIDN'T KNOW MYSELF.

Any man can be a father. It takes someone special to be a dad.

ANONYMOUS

EVEN WHEN WE HAD OUR DIFFERENCES, THEY ONLY HIGHLIGHTED OUR SIMILARITIES.

I STILL HAVE THE BOOKS YOU GAVE ME. ONE DAY I MAY EVEN READ THEM!

When I lost my sense of direction, you were always there with a compass.

YOUR ATTEMPTS TO UNDERSTAND ME AS A TEENAGER MADE ME LAUGH, BUT I'M SO PROUD THAT YOU CARED ENOUGH TO TRY.

A father is a man who expects his children to be as good as he meant to be.

FRANK A CLARK

YOU CELEBRATED MY GROWTH AND INCREASING INDEPENDENCE, EVEN THOUGH IT MUST HAVE BEEN DIFFICULT TO LET GO.

Some of your jokes make me groan, but now I want to make others groan to them as well.

Sometimes I think you're completely crazy – and then I'm glad you are.

One of my favourite things to do in the world is make you laugh.

YOU MADE ME LAUGH AT MY MISTAKES AND LEARN NOT TO TAKE MYSELF TOO SERIOUSLY.

Your laughter can drive all the discontent from my heart.

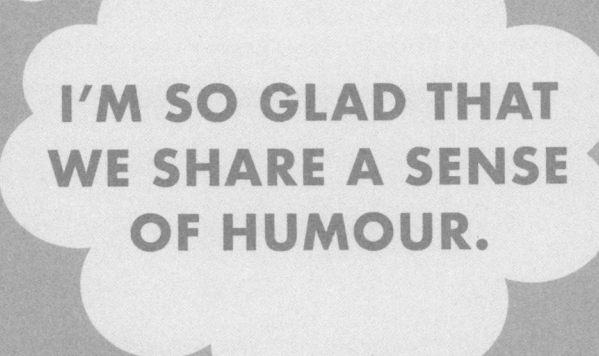

I'M SO GLAD THAT WE SHARE A SENSE OF HUMOUR.

Sometimes our eyes meet and we burst into spontaneous laughter that no outsider could ever understand.

YOUR WHOLEHEARTED LAUGHTER MADE ME BELIEVE THAT MY SILLY JOKES WERE FUNNY AND THAT I WAS A TRUE COMEDIAN.

I love to hear funny stories about the mischief you made when you were young.

Somehow you had a sixth sense that told you when my shrieks were from fear and when they were from delight.

YOUR FEARLESSNESS HELPED ME TO OVERCOME MY OWN FEARS.

You never laughed at me when it would have hurt my pride.

You taught me that laughter can often be the best medicine.

Every thing in this world, said my father, is big with jest, and has wit in it, and instruction too, if we can but find it out.

LAURENCE STERNE

You always gave me what I needed, even when I didn't know what it was.

EVEN IF I CAME LAST IN THE RACE, I CAME IN TO A HERO'S WELCOME.

Dads are stone skimmers, mud wallowers, water wallopers, ceiling swoopers, shoulder gallopers, upsy-downsy, over-and-through, round-and-about whooshers.

HELEN THOMSON

I'VE ALWAYS KNOWN

I CAN TELL YOU

ANYTHING.

You understood that being there is the first step to being a good dad.

You made my world a magical place.

You always had an idea that could entertain me.

You didn't mind when I jumped in puddles and splashed my clothes – or yours.

FORGET CLARK KENT – TO ME YOU WERE THE REAL SUPERMAN.

You showed an interest in everything that interested me, no matter how mundane it might have seemed to you.

You lifted me high in the air and gave me a new perspective on the world.

YOU ENCOURAGED MISCHIEF, AS LONG AS IT WASN'T CRUEL.

YOU MADE THE RULES BUT WERE OFTEN WILLING TO BEND THEM.

> **YOU WERE NEVER TOO OLD TO GET DOWN ON YOUR HANDS AND KNEES AND PLAY.**

I love remembering the games we used to play on long journeys.

My father used to play with my brother and me in the yard. Mother would come out and say, "You're tearing up the grass." "We're not raising grass," my dad would reply, "We're raising boys."

HARMON KILLEBREW

THE THINGS YOU TAUGHT ME EQUIPPED ME TO GO OUT INTO THE WORLD AS A CONFIDENT ADULT.

> You taught me to hold out for real love in life.

YOU WERE THE SOURCE OF ALL THE BEST GAMES, AND YOU KNEW ALL THE RULES.

Holidays were always fun and memorable, thanks to you.

WE ALWAYS LAUGHED AT EACH OTHER WITH AFFECTION.

YOU CAN DO A VERY FUNNY IMITATION OF ME.

You taught me to look and listen, to think and question.

You were never too proud to look something up, to be sure you were giving me the right information.

You let me choose my own path, and you never made me believe I'd taken the wrong one.

YOU TAUGHT ME NEVER TO SAY, "I CAN'T", UNLESS I'D TRIED

You made sure I had plenty of time to play

One father is more than a hundred schoolmasters.

SEVENTEENTH-CENTURY ENGLISH PROVERB

You were strict when you needed to be but I always knew you were fair.

I KNEW THAT YOU HAD RULES BECAUSE YOU LOVED ME AND WANTED ME TO BE SAFE.

You taught me that good manners open doors in life.

To show a child what has once delighted you, to find the child's delight added to your own so that there is now a double delight seen in the glow of trust and affection, this is happiness.

J B PRIESTLEY

YOU ALWAYS SHOWED ME THAT IF I THOUGHT THINGS THROUGH, THE ANSWER WOULD COME TO ME.

YOU'VE HELPED ME TO TREASURE THE SIMPLE THINGS IN LIFE.

You taught me that it didn't matter if I won or lost, as long as I tried my best.

I talk and talk and talk, and I haven't taught people in fifty years what my father taught by example in one week.

MARIO CUOMO

THE BEST LESSONS WERE THE ONES YOU DIDN'T EVEN KNOW YOU WERE TEACHING ME.

YOUR TRUST IN ME

MADE ME TRUST

IN MYSELF.

When you refused me something, I knew it had to be for a good reason.

YOU MADE SURE THAT OUR HOME WAS FULL OF STIMULATING BOOKS AND PICTURES TO HELP ME LEARN.

You were almost always right – much to my frustration.

YOU TAUGHT ME TO VALUE THE LESSONS OF THE PAST.

You always took the time to explain things properly.

YOU SHOWED ME HOW STORIES CAN BRING THE WORLD ALIVE.

From you, I learned a strong sense of fairness.

By the time a man realizes that maybe his father was right, he usually has a son who thinks he's wrong.

CHARLES WADSWORTH

YOU TAUGHT ME THE POWER THAT WORDS CAN HAVE, AND HOW TO USE THEM WISELY.

YOU SHOWED ME HOW TO RESERVE JUDGMENT UNTIL I KNEW ALL THE FACTS.

I could never go wrong by copying your example.

I learned from you that it is worth looking at both sides of an argument.

You taught me that sometimes it's right to let the other person win.

My father always told me, "Find a job you love and you'll never have to work a day in your life."

JIM FOX

You helped me let go of the idea that I always had to be right.

YOU MADE ME SEE THAT THERE IS MORE THAN ONE FORM OF SUCCESS.

You've shown me that
hard work is important
and worthwhile.

**You made sure that
I wasn't afraid to
speak up for myself.**

**You showed me early on that
it's always best to talk about
things that bother me.**

YOU TRIED TO MAKE SURE I UNDERSTOOD THE DIFFERENCE BETWEEN RIGHT AND WRONG.

WHEN I MADE MISTAKES, YOU TALKED THEM THROUGH WITH ME.

You taught me to count my blessings when I'm feeling low.

> **You made sure I was independent enough to cope on my own when I needed to.**

Your high expectations of me made me expect the most from myself.

My father had taught me – mostly by example – that if a man wanted to be in charge of his life, he had to be in charge of his problems.

STEPHEN KING

You taught me to accept defeat with grace.

My dreams became yours, and you inspired me to chase them with you.

I ALWAYS FELT GUIDED BY YOUR PRINCIPLES.

If I had a question, you always seemed to have an answer.

You made me treasure the ability to be independent.

Who else would treasure all the paintings I brought home from school as if they were Picassos?

YOU'VE ALWAYS INSISTED I SHOULD BE KIND AND CONSIDERATE TO EVERYONE, AND TO EXPECT THE SAME IN RETURN.

He who is taught to live upon little owes more to his father's wisdom than he who has a great deal left him does to his father's care.

WILLIAM PENN

You taught me to value common sense and my own instincts.

You made sure I was excited by new opportunities.

My father taught me that the only way you can make good at anything is to practice, and then practice some more.

PETE ROSE

YOU HELPED ME UNDERSTAND THAT TEARS ARE NOTHING TO BE ASHAMED OF.

You showed me that I need to take risks sometimes.

YOU MADE ME REALIZE THAT IF BAD TIMES COME, GOOD TIMES WILL AS WELL.

Fathers, like mothers, are not born. Men grow into fathers, and fathering is a very important stage in their development.

DAVID GOTTESMAN

> **You helped me to recognize my talents and make the most of them.**

Words have an awesome impact. The impressions made by my father's voice can set in motion an entire trend of life.

GORDON MACDONALD

> You made sure I knew the value of money and how to look after my finances.

My dad always used to tell me that if they challenge you to an after-school fight, tell them you won't wait – you can kick their ass right now.

CAMERON DIAZ

You can tell when I don't want advice, and you usually manage to bite your tongue.

YOU WERE NEVER TOO TIRED OR BORED FOR PLAY.

You made sure I understood how rewarding a career can be, but not at the expense of everything else.

YOU NEVER SPOILED ME WITH TOO MANY POSSESSIONS, BUT GAVE ME ALL THE LOVE I NEEDED.

You never lost your patience when I couldn't grasp what you were teaching me.

> **YOU TAUGHT ME WHAT IT MEANS TO BE A GOOD PERSON IN THE WORLD.**

When you said no, you always meant it.

From the reputation and remembrance of my father, [I learned] modesty and a manly character.

MARCUS AURELIUS

YOU SHOWED ME THAT MATERIAL SUCCESS IS HOLLOW IF IT COMES AT THE EXPENSE OF LOVE.

I cherish every moment we have together, because life is unpredictable.

You made sure I wasn't afraid to stand up and be counted.

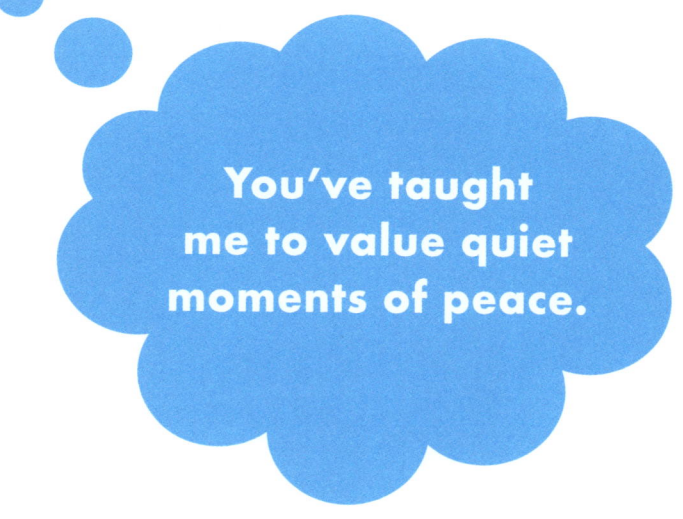

You've taught me to value quiet moments of peace.

I learned from you that there is more than one right way to do things.

He taught me all I needed to know about faith and hard work by the simple eloquence of his example.

MARIO CUOMO

You wanted me to be well educated for my benefit, not because it reflected well on you.

The best and wisest man I ever knew, who taught me many lessons and showed me many things as we went together along the country by-ways.

SARAH ORNE JEWETT

YOU SHOWED ME I'M NOT HELPLESS – THAT THERE'S ALWAYS A WAY TO GET THINGS DONE.

You made me realize that it's never too late to say, "I'm sorry," or "I love you."

YOU TAUGHT ME THAT THERE IS A DIFFERENCE BETWEEN TAKING A RISK AND BEING RECKLESS.

You taught me that I can achieve whatever I want in life if I work hard enough.

YOU MAKE ME FEEL THAT FATHERHOOD IS YOUR PROUDEST ACHIEVEMENT.

Everything I ever learned as a small boy came from my father. And I never found anything he ever told me to be wrong or worthless.

IRVING PICHEL

You taught me to walk, and in more ways than one, you guided my first steps.

I'LL ALWAYS REMEMBER THE WAY YOU DIDN'T LIKE TO MISS ANYTHING.

A man's children and his garden both reflect the amount of weeding done during the growing season.

ANONYMOUS

You taught me to take what life throws at me with good grace.

> **YOU REMEMBER EXACTLY WHERE ALL MY BABY PICTURES WERE TAKEN.**

The best way of training the young is to train yourself at the same time; not to admonish them, but to be seen never doing that of which you would admonish them.

PLATO

WHEN I WAS A CHILD, YOU WERE MY FATHER; NOW THAT I'M GROWN UP, YOU ARE MY FRIEND AS WELL.

You've always been
interested in what
I have to say.

**It makes me proud
when people tell me
how much they like you.**

Only a father doesn't
begrudge his son's talent.

JOHANN WOLFGANG VON GOETHE

**YOU REMEMBER THINGS
I TELL YOU ABOUT PEOPLE
YOU'VE NEVER MET.**

When I've been at my lowest,
you've always been there.

**YOUR APPROVAL
IS ALWAYS WORTH
STRIVING FOR.**

I save up things to tell you that
I know you'll be interested in.

WHEN I NEEDED TO TALK, YOU LISTENED.

You tell me the truth, even when I don't want to hear it.

YOUR GENEROSITY TO MY FRIENDS MAKES ME PROUD TO BRING THEM HOME.

YOU'VE ALWAYS SPOKEN TO ME AS AN EQUAL.

It is much easier to become a father than to be one.

KENT NERBURN

You made me understand that friendship between parent and child is not only possible, but magical.

WHEN I CALL HOME, MY SPIRITS LIFT WHEN YOU ANSWER THE PHONE.

Wherever you are, you always take the time to make sure that I'm OK.

There was always time to sit down, talk, and laugh.

YOU NEVER PUSHED ME TO BE ANYTHING OTHER THAN I AM.

A shaky child on a bicycle for the first time needs both support and freedom.

SLOAN WILSON

YOU SHOWED ME THAT I SHOULD THINK THE BEST OF OTHER PEOPLE.

The words that a father speaks to his children in the privacy of home are not heard by the world, but, as in whispering galleries, they are clearly heard at the end, and by posterity.

JEAN PAUL RICHTER

I know that I will never find my father in any other man who comes into my life, because it is a void in my life that can only be filled by him.

HALLE BERRY

YOU'VE GOT NO IDEA HOW OFTEN I BEGIN A SENTENCE WITH THE PHRASE, "MY DAD SAYS..."

You were always kind to my friends, and I was proud to have them meet you.

I am many things besides, but I am Daddy's girl and so I will remain – all the way to the old folks' home.

PAULA WEIDEGER

I believe that what we become depends on what our fathers teach us at odd moments, when they aren't trying to teach us. We are formed by little scraps of wisdom.

UMBERTO ECO

Your father knows what you need before you ask him.

MATTHEW 6:8

You were the hub of our home, the centre we revolved around.

You were generous with your time as well as your money.

YOU KNEW ME BETTER THAN I KNEW MYSELF.

You had such an air of competence, I never realized when you didn't know what you were doing.

YOU'D DO ANYTHING TO MAKE ME HAPPY, BUT YOU NEVER LET ME WRAP YOU AROUND MY LITTLE FINGER.

A king, realizing his incompetence, can either delegate or abdicate his duties. A father can do neither. If only sons could see the paradox, they would understand the dilemma.

MARLENE DIETRICH

WHEN YOUR FAVOURITE SONGS COME ON THE RADIO, I SMILE AND THINK OF YOU.

A father is a guy who has snapshots in his wallet where his money used to be.

ANONYMOUS

Father is rather vulgar, my dear. The word Papa, besides, gives a very, pretty form to the lips.

CHARLES DICKENS

You were good at answering questions like "why is the sky blue?" and "why do bees sting?"

A sunny morning always filled you with good humour and now it does the same for me.

YOU'VE SHOWN ME THE COMFORT OF AN EVENING SPENT IN FRONT OF THE FIRE WITH A GOOD BOOK.

THESE DAYS I CATCH MYSELF USING SOME OF YOUR FAVOURITE PHRASES AND SAYINGS, MORE THAN YOU WOULD BELIEVE!

Some day you will know that a father is much happier in his children's happiness than in his own. I cannot explain it to you: it is a feeling in your body that spreads gladness through you.

HONORÉ DE BALZAC

SOMETIMES YOU LOOKED THE OTHER WAY WHEN YOU HAD EVERY RIGHT TO BE ANGRY.

You never mind silence when we are together; our closeness speaks more than words.

You understood that life is sweeter with the occasional treat.

Where there was a problem, you found a solution.

You help me see that love and relationships are the most valuable things of all.

A father is a banker provided by nature.
FRENCH PROVERB

YOU'RE THE ONE WHO WAS ALWAYS ABLE TO MAKE THE NIGHTMARES GO AWAY.

THE WORLD WOULDN'T FEEL LIKE SUCH A SAFE PLACE WITHOUT YOU IN IT.

You took your role as a father seriously, but with tenderness.

Even when we're far apart, I find comfort knowing that you're thinking about me.

I KNOW THAT NO MATTER HOW MUCH TIME PASSES OR HOW FAR I TRAVEL, THERE'S ALWAYS A PLACE FOR ME AT HOME.

When I face a problem I still think to myself, 'What would Dad do?'

ON YOUR SHOULDERS, ANCHORED BY YOUR STEADY GRIP, I COULD LOOK OUT AT THE WORLD LIKE A GIANT.

My dear father! When I remember him, it is always with his arms open wide to love and comfort me.

ISOBEL FIELD

After a day of falls, bumps, and mishaps, you gave me the familiar comfort of your arms and made me feel safe again.

How sweetie it is to sit 'neath a fond father's smile.

JOHN HOWARD PAYNE

You made sure I had the confidence to stand up and be heard.

> **And how my father loved and watched us, and guarded our happiness.**
>
> EDGAR LEE MASTERS

When I faced tough times, I knew you were right behind me.

I OWE YOU SO MUCH,
BUT YOU NEVER
MAKE ME FEEL IT.

YOU SHOWED ME THAT NO TROUBLE IS SO BAD THAT IT CAN'T BE OVERCOME.

YOU TAUGHT ME THAT I COULD RELY ON MYSELF.

You made me confident that there was a happy ending waiting for me.

You gave me a home that was full of warmth, light, and laughter.

YOU WIPED MY TEARS, BANDAGED MY WOUNDS, AND MADE ME REALIZE THAT I COULD TRY AGAIN.

[He] adopted a role called Being a Father so that his child would have something mythical and infinitely important: a Protector, who would keep a lid on all the chaotic and catastrophic possibilities of life.

TOM WOLFE

YOU WERE THERE, MY HERO, FOR EVERY LITTLE THING I NEEDED.

YOU TELL ME NOT TO WORRY ABOUT THINGS THAT MIGHT NEVER HAPPEN.

I could never have taken the risks I've taken in my life if I didn't know I had you there as a safety net.

Safe, for a child, is his father's hand, holding him tight.

MARION C GARRETTY

You made me believe you could do anything – and through that, I believed I could, too.

When you threw me high in the air, I never doubted for a second that you would catch me.

My father died many years ago, and yet when something special happens to me, I talk to him secretly, not really knowing whether he hears, but it makes me feel better to half believe it.

NATASHA JOSEFOWITZ

WHATEVER LIFE THROWS AT YOU, I KNOW YOU WILL BE CAPABLE OF HANDLING IT.

You always had time to sit down and work through a problem with me.

AFTER A TRIP YOU ALWAYS WANT ME TO PHONE TO LET YOU KNOW I'VE MADE IT HOME SAFELY. EVEN IF I COMPLAIN, SECRETLY, IT MAKES ME FEEL SECURE.

I cannot think of any need in childhood as strong as the need for a father's protection.

SIGMUND FREUD

The thing to remember about fathers is, they're men. A girl has to keep it in mind: They are dragon-seekers, bent on improbable rescues.

PHYLLIS MCGINLEY

Dads are most ordinary men turned by love into heroes, adventurers, story-tellers, and singers of song.

PAM BROWN

You showed me how to see the light at the end of the tunnel.

All about him was safe.

NAOMI MITCHISON

'DAD' IS SUCH A SMALL WORD, WHEN YOU THINK OF ALL THE BIG EMOTIONS THAT GO WITH IT.

YOU CHASED AWAY

THE MONSTERS

UNDER MY BED.

You always told me I could do anything and go anywhere, and that broadened my horizons.

You've always had complete faith in me, even when I've felt low and useless.

You've always inspired me with your enthusiasm for everything life has to offer.

YOU'RE ALWAYS EXCITED ABOUT THE THINGS I ACHIEVE IN LIFE.

My mother and father are the only people on the whole planet for whom I will never begrudge a thing. Should I achieve great things, it is the work of their hands.

ANTON CHEKHOV

YOU GAVE ME THE FOUNDATION I NEEDED FOR A WELL-BALANCED LIFE.

You made me realize that there is no substitute for a happy childhood and a loving family.

You taught me that as long as I am happy with myself, I will lead a satisfied life.

You used your hands, your mind, and your heart to show me the world.

You made sure I was able to hold on to the magic of childhood for as long as possible.

YOU OPENED THE DOORS OF MY IMAGINATION.

YOU NEVER TRIED TO CHANGE JUST TO PLEASE OTHERS.

My father instilled in me that if you don't see things happening the way you want them to, you get out there and make them happen.

SUSAN POWTER

YOUR PRIDE IN ME MADE ME BELIEVE IN MYSELF.

YOU MADE ME REALIZE THAT ONE PERSON CAN DEFINITELY MAKE A DIFFERENCE IN THE WORLD.

If the relationship of father to son could really be reduced to biology, the whole earth would blaze with the glory of fathers and sons.

JAMES BALDWIN

Your inquisitive mind made me want to ask questions, too.

You made me think that there were no limits to what I could achieve.

YOU OPENED MY EYES TO SO MUCH THE WORLD HAS TO OFFER.

When I was a kid, my father told me every day, "You're the most wonderful boy in the world, and you can do anything you want to."

JAN HUTCHINS

You showed me that the smartest people are the ones who know how much they still have to learn.

You would never make fun of my ambitions or tell me they're unrealistic.

My father gave me the greatest gift anyone could give another person: he believed in me.

JIM VALVANO

One man with courage makes a majority.

ANDREW JACKSON

IF I AMOUNT TO ANYTHING, IT'S BECAUSE OF YOU.

Let my father's honours live in me.

WILLIAM SHAKESPEARE

YOU MADE ME INTERESTED IN THE THINGS YOU ARE PASSIONATE ABOUT.

YOU WERE THE MAKING OF ME – YOU WERE SO TRUE TO ME AND SO SURE OF ME.

The older I get, the more of you I see in myself, and I like what I see.

YOU'VE ALWAYS EMBRACED THE NEW, AND SHOWN ME HOW TO AS WELL.

If people tell me I'm a good person, I know the credit is yours.

You trusted me to go places alone, and that gave me courage.

YOU MADE ME REALIZE THAT LIFE WILL ALWAYS HAVE PITFALLS, AND THAT THEY ARE TO BE OVERCOME, NOT FEARED.

You've taught me to be a dreamer with my feet on the ground.

You taught me to join in with the singing, even if I didn't know the words.

YOU'VE MADE ME FEEL THAT EVERYTHING IS WITHIN MY REACH.

My father did enough in his lifetime to answer for both of us.

WOODROW WILSON

YOU DIDN'T LAUGH AT MY CRAZY FANTASIES OF WHAT I WANTED TO DO WITH MY LIFE.

Directly after God in heaven comes Papa.

WOLFGANG AMADEUS MOZART

Because of you, the word 'father' is full of warmth for me.

You convinced me that I'm special.

IT'S NOT MUCH TO SAY, BUT – THANK YOU.

YOU MADE ME BELIEVE THAT I WAS WORTHY OF BEING LOVED.

Did I mention that I loved you?